CIM

Mar

Maggi

ELSEV

AMSTER

PARIS

Butterworth-Heinemann is an imprint of Elsevier
Linacre House, Jordan Hill, Oxford OX2 8DP
30 Corporate Drive, Suite 400, Burlington, MA 01803

First published 2006

British Library Cataloguing in Publication Data
A catalogue record for this book is available from the British Library

ISBN-13: 978 0 7506 8283 1
ISBN-10: 0 7506 8283 3

For information on all Elsevier Butterworth-Heinemann publications visit our website at http://books.elsevier.com

Printed and bound in Great Britain

06 07 08 09 10   10 9 8 7 6 5 4 3 2 1

TABLE OF CONTENTS

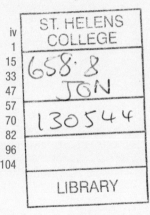

PREFACE

Welcome to the CIM Revision Cards from Elsevier/Butterworth-Heinemann. We hope you will find these useful to revise for your CIM exam. The cards are designed to be used in conjunction with the CIM Coursebooks from Elsevier/Butterworth-Heinemann, and have been written specifically with revision in mind. They also serve as invaluable reviews of the complete modules, perfect for those studying via the assignment route.

- Learning outcomes at the start of each chapter identify the main points
- Key topics are summarized, helping you commit the information to memory quickly and easily
- Examination and revision tips are provided to give extra guidance when preparing for the exam
- Key diagrams are featured to aid the learning process
- The compact size ensures the cards are easily transportable, so you can revise any time, anywhere

To get the most of your revision cards, try to look over them as frequently as you can when taking your CIM course. When read alongside the Coursebook they serve as the ideal companion to the main text.

Good luck – we wish you every success with your CIM qualification!

THE DEVELOPMENT OF MARKETING AND MARKETING ORIENTATION

LEARNING OUTCOMES

➡ Understanding the development of marketing as an exchange process and a business philosophy

➡ Recognizing the contribution of marketing to create customer value and compete effectively

➡ Appreciate the importance of marketing orientation and identify the factors that promote and impede its adoption

➡ Understand the role of marketing in coordinating organizational resources

➡ Understand the impact of marketing actions upon society and the need to act in a socially responsible manner

➡ Appreciate the significance of the buyer–seller relationship and the role of relationship marketing in retaining customers

Syllabus Reference: 1.1–1.6

KEY REVISION POINTS

➥ The importance of a marketing orientated culture to the effective implementation of marketing strategies within the organization

➥ Understanding the dynamics of the buyer– seller relationship across a range of industry sectors

➥ Understanding the role of ICT in further development of marketing orientation

➥ The importance of internal marketing in building and sustaining a marketing culture within the organization

What is Marketing?

The management process which identifies, anticipates and satisfies customer requirements efficiently and profitably

- Central focus is the customer
- Aim is to satisfy their needs
- Encompasses selling, researching markets and attracting and retaining customers
- Requires a set of management activities to be in place to enable organization to compete

Marketing is about creating a mutually beneficial exchange (Dibb et al.) determined by the following

- Two parties must participate
- Each party must possess something of value
- Both parties must be willing to exchange
- Usually involves exchanging money for goods and services

The Marketing Concept puts the customer at the centre of all business decision-making. An organization with this approach is said to be marketing orientated to have a marketing culture

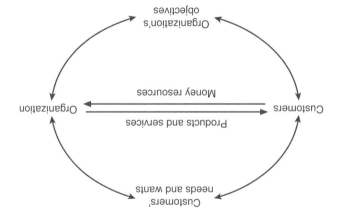

The Development of Marketing Orientation

1900–1930 Production Orientation – focused on what the organization can produce, not if there is a need for what can be produced

1930–1960 Selling Orientation – focused on persuading customers to buy through using selling and promotion

1960–present day Marketing Orientation – identifies what the customer wants and attempts to satisfy those needs better than the competition and within the organizational capabilities

Marketing Culture – the first step to developing a marketing culture within an organization is to ensure all employees at all levels and functions have the ability and information to **'think customers'**

Factors underpinning further development

- Customers are better educated and knowledgeable, exercising more power
- Higher disposable income available
- Overcapacity of goods and services
- Emergence of global brands via better traveled customers and increased information
- Better quality information enables closer segmentation and targeting of key customer groups
- Increased channels to market – especially on-line

Creating a Sustainable Competitive Advantage

Marketing orientation can enable the organization to compete by

- Creating and maintaining superior value through effective application of the marketing mix
- Creating a link between customer needs and organizational strengths
- Consider the competition from the customer perspective

Organizational Factors Required for Marketing Culture to Flourish

- Committed senior management
- Specific board level marketing responsibility
- Customer satisfaction inherent in all job descriptions
- Training in customer care for all
- Training in marketing developments for marketing staff
- Reward and motivation systems in place
- Regular marketing research

Internal Marketing to Create a Marketing Culture

Key Definition – The creation of an internal environment which supports customer consciousness and sales-mindedness amongst all personnel within an organization

Benefits

- More profitable organizations
- Increasing need for jobs and staff development
- Greater job satisfaction possible
- Better skilled, empowered employees

Internal marketing must demonstrate and communicate

- The organizational objectives and strategies within the markets they compete in
- The importance to the organization of delivering superior customer value
- The rewards available through implementing successful strategies
- How all employees contribute to the customer experience
- An understanding of the differing needs and requirements of differing employee groups
- How improving customer care improves job satisfaction and motivation

Barriers to Implementing a Marketing Culture

■ Failure of managers to understand and embrace a marketing culture

■ Resistance to change

■ Political power struggles between the organization's functions and departments

■ Lack of clearly defined responsibility for internal marketing

■ Organizational structure may inhibit two-way communication and dissemination of information

Marketing Must Play a Coordinating Role

Customers

↑↓

Marketing functions/activities

↑↓

Other internal company functions/activities

↑↓

External factors/activities

Wider Application of Marketing Culture

The marketing environment is dynamic and ever changing

Marketing has spread from the FMCG sectors and is now prevalent in many other industry sectors

Business-to-Business (B2B)

Purchasing on behalf of the organization rather than for personal use. Key relationships between supplier, manufacturers and distributors to deliver added value to the end user. Buying decision-making process (DMP) is longer and involves more people (decision making unit, DMU)

Service Industries

Dominate in many developed economies such as USA and UK. Key issues are Intangibility, Inseparability and Perishability of the service offered. Benefits much more difficult to communicate

Not-for-Profit

These organizations exist for reasons other than to produce profit and are often service based, e.g. hospitals, universities and charities. Usually have to operate within a tight regulatory framework and the 'customers' are numerous and have very different and often conflicting needs

Global Marketing

The emergence of a global village. Customers around the world have similar lifestyles and consumption patterns to their global neighbours. Increased mobility and education of consumers, aligned with more efficient communication, has led to the growth of global brands

Further Developments

Relationship Marketing

Aims to maximize the value generated from the buyer–seller exchange by establishing a longer-term relationship and brand loyal customers. Database technology has enabled tracking of purchases and targeted communication. Focus on increasing Customer Lifetime Value–(CLV)

Quality and Customer Care

Arises from the need to build relationships. Marketing has recognized that customers perceive quality and level of customer care delivered as a differentiating factor when purchasing. More powerful consumers now expect and demand consistent quality and service

Societal Marketing

Organizations have become more environmentally aware in response to customers becoming more discerning. The possible effect of marketing activities and provision of goods and services on society and the environment are also key differentiators in the minds of more and more customers. More organizations developing a stance on Corporate Social Responsibility (CSR)

Database Marketing

Increased information availability and channels of communication via ICT have led to better segmentation, shorter time to market and increased channels to market. Flexibility has led to greater differentiation in product/service offering

Marketing as a Management Function

Key steps in marketing planning

Business mission/corporate objectives

↓

Marketing audit

↓

SWOT analysis

↓

Business objectives

↓

Marketing objectives

↓

Marketing strategies

↓

Marketing tactics/marketing mix decisions

↓

Implementation

↓

Monitoring and control

Key Tasks of the Marketing Manager

Analysis – Assessment of

Micro factors – Customers, competition, supply chain, other stakeholders

Macro factors – Legal, social, economic, technological, political, environmental

Planning – Process detailed on the left

Implementation – Ensuring budgets and resources (e.g. staff) are in place to implement the plan and the plans are communicated and accepted

Control – Measuring the effectiveness of the plan implemented in relation to achievement of objectives set. Changed circumstances may lead to plans being amended. Process continues on to the next planning cycle

Marketing Mix – Tools of Marketing Management

Key Definition – The marketing mix is the set of controllable variables which the marketer uses to develop marketing plans and programmes

Basic 4Ps – As developed by Neil Borden	**The Extended/Service Mix – 7Ps**

Product	Process
Price	People
Place	Physical Evidence
Promotion	

Growth of Technology in Marketing

Helps with the development of a marketing-orientated culture by

- Using sophisticated databases to understand Customer Behaviour
- Using the Internet to gather competitor information
- Building customer care systems
- Identifying segments and niches with differing needs
- Communicating with customers in a more direct way
- Gathering information to underpin effective marketing planning and decision-making

Major Effects on the Marketing Environment include

- Growth of home shopping
- Greater price competition as customers can compare prices via the Internet – price transparency
- Potential demise of some markets to be replaced by new products and industries
- New relationships and level of interaction between members of the value chain

Hints and Tips

■ Read through Unit 1 of the Marketing Fundamentals Coursebook – these revision tips relate closely to it

■ The Marketing Fundamentals exam is about being able to apply a range of concepts and theories in the context of an organization

■ You need to show the examiner that you can understand how to 'do marketing'!

■ Introduce different theories to underpin your answers

■ Use as many process models as possible to help you remember key concepts

■ Challenge theories where you think they may not be appropriate or where you think they could be disproven

■ Use examples to support your answers where appropriate – e.g. egg, easyJet, Starbucks…

■ Answer the question asked!

■ Break down the different components of the questions to ensure you address all of the issues

■ Have a go at as many past exam questions as possible

■ Go to www.cimvirtualinstitute.com and www.marketingonline.co.uk for additional support and guidance

MARKETING PLANNING AND BUDGETING

LEARNING OUTCOMES

➡ Understanding the importance of the planning process and the structure and stages of the marketing plan

➡ Understanding the models available in the audit and strategy formulation stages of the marketing plan

➡ Understanding the importance of objective setting, market segmentation and the value of marketing research to the planning process

➡ Appreciate the range of tools and techniques available to satisfy customer needs and compete effectively

➡ Understand the process of setting marketing budgets

KEY REVISION POINTS

➡ The relationship between the marketing plan and the corporate plan

➡ What are the basics of a good marketing strategy?

➡ The role and components of the marketing plan and barriers to marketing planning

Syllabus Reference: 2.1–2.11, 3.1, 3.16

Why Plan?

More organizations now undertake a structured planning process because:

- The marketing environment is highly competitive and change is occurring at a rapid rate
- High levels of investment are required to develop new products and services
- More sophisticated planning techniques and tools are available
- Marketing personnel are better trained and have access to better quality data and information
- Organizations recognize the need to integrate all functions of the organization to better meet the customers needs

The advantages are:

- A structured analysis of the environment the organization operates within is undertaken
- Objectives and strategies are based on the strengths and resources available
- Proactive approach rather than a reactive one enables the organization to compete better
- Increased customer focus possible
- Better use of organizational resources

The Planning Process

See Unit 1 for the extended process, but more simply

M.A.O.S.T.I.C.

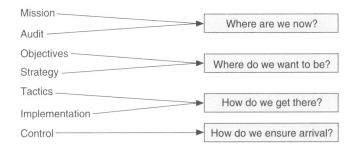

Mission ———————→ Where are we now?
Audit ———————→

Objectives ———————→ Where do we want to be?
Strategy ———————→

Tactics ———————→ How do we get there?
Implementation ———————→

Control ———————→ How do we ensure arrival?

Marketing in the context of the organization

Marketing plays a role in feeding information upwards to provide guidance, direction and vision for the corporate objectives and the development of the corporate strategy, as shown in the Strategy and Planning Hierarchy below

■ Corporate planning starts at the top of the organization and impinges upon every aspect and every division or department of the organization

■ Corporate strategy and plans are clearly linked to achieving the mission and vision of the organization

■ Each business unit has responsibility for the development of its own function plans

Corporate Strategy

Mission and vision of the organization
Corporate objectives
Business strategy
Resource requirements and deployment
Corporate value systems – corporate planning

Operations
finance,
HRM
functions

Corporate objectives
cascade through to all
organizational
functions

Marketing
function,
Marketing
objectives
and marketing
strategy

Marketing Tactics
Objectives
The marketing mix
Marketing activites

Understanding the stages in more detail

Mission – What business are we in? What are our values?

Objectives – Need to be SMART. Focus on growth, financial performance, reputation and corporate social responsibility (CSR)

Audit – Should encompass all aspects of the organization and the environment it operates within

Assessment of skills, resources and systems, the organization use to develop a sustainable competitive advantage (SCA). See SWOT

Internal/Micro-Competitors	Customers
Distributors	Suppliers
External/Macro-Legal	Political
Economic	Technological
Social	Environmental

Objectives – Provide the guiding framework on how the company will compete in a market place. Should relate to:

> Market share
>
> Market scope – range of products/services
>
> Innovation – NPD
>
> Positioning in the minds of consumers
>
> Market position in relation to competitors

Strategy – see below

Implementation – detailing the actions required to bring the Marketing Plan to life. Include:

Men	Materials
Money	Minutes
Machines	

Control – Measurement vs. objectives

How the SWOT Analysis Helps the Planning Process

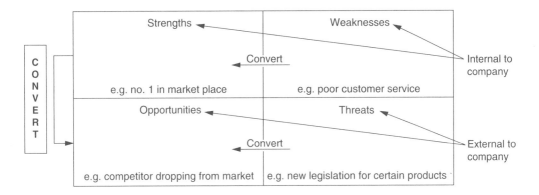

Strategy Formulation – Useful Tools – Ansoff's Growth Matrix

	Current products	New products
Current markets	Market penetration strategy	Product development strategy
New markets	Market development strategy	Diversification strategy

Market Penetration – existing customers buy more or encourage brand switching from competition

Market Development – enter new market segments, e.g. International or geographic areas

Product Development – develop additional features or additions to range. Enter new product areas

Diversification – most risky, can be in related or non-related areas, e.g. CAT clothing

Porter's Three Generic Competitive Strategies

As developed by Michael Porter

Cost Leadership – The ability to compete on price due to market position or organizational efficiencies

Focus/Niche – Meeting the needs of a small, closely targeted sector

Differentiation – Meeting a set of specific customer needs more closely

Marketing segmentation and competitive positioning

SEGMENTATION
Consider the basis on which to segment the market – geographic, demographic, geo-demographic, lifestyle, behavioural. Look at the profile of people and how they break into groups and confirm if the groups are valid segments

TARGETING
Decide on target strategy
Decide which segments should be targeted and why?

POSITIONING
Understand consumer perceptions
Position products in the mind of the consumer
Design an appropriate marketing mix to achieve that positioning and meet customer requirements

Stages in Marketing Segmentation Process

■ *Identify the possible segments within the market* – this will consist of individuals or organizations with similar needs or preferences

■ *Gather information on those market segments identified* – to do this, the segments need to be accessible

■ *Evaluate the attractiveness of different segments* – they need to be large enough to be viable

■ *Ascertain the competitive position within each of the target segments*

■ *Develop variations on product/service specifications to meet the needs of individual segments*

■ *Design the appropriate communications mix to meet the target market demands*

REMEMBER! 🖎

1. Customers must need and want the products/ services

2. Customers must assert their buying power, i.e. money, resources, etc.

3. Customers must be willing to use their money and resources to buy products

4. Customers must have authority to buy different products or services!

Basis for Segmentation

Any basis used must be:

- Measurable
- Substantial
- Accessible

Consumer Bases	Industrial Bases
Demographics	Industry type
Socioeconomic	Size of the organization
Geographic	Geographic
Personality and lifestyle	User status
Frequency of use	Usage rate
Benefits sought	Benefits sought

Targeting as a Marketing Activity

Options for deciding on target markets include:

- Organizations should concentrate on making one product for one market and having one marketing plan – i.e. *mass marketing*

- The organization could concentrate its efforts on one market but have a number of different versions of each product – *differentiated marketing*

- Concentrating efforts on a small and carefully chosen segment – *focus market*

Six components of target marketing

1. Customer needs – wants and expectations
2. Product market – size and structure
3. Brand strength and market share
4. Company capability
5. Competitive rivalry
6. Economies of scale – production and marketing

Positioning as a Marketing Activity

Steps in establishing a positioning plan

- Identify all segments within the market
- Decide which segments are most suitable
- Ensure the organization understands customer requirements
- Develop product or service that specifically meets the target audience needs
- Identify benefits, usage, user category, competitive positioning

- Evaluate how the product or service is positioned in the eyes of the target group
- Identify an image that matches the requirements of the customer
- Promote the product to the target audience, establish relationships and aim for customer loyalty

Remember positioning alternatives

- *Distinctive*
- *Fill the gaps*
- *Repositioning*

Tactics – The Development of the Marketing Mix

The application of the 4/7Ps to the organizational context. See Unit 1

Contextualization is the key to ensure these elements are brought together to form an integrated and cohesive whole

Synergy

Where the outcome of combining the individual elements of the marketing mix together is greater than the simple sum total of each of the elements. Often expressed as $2 + 2 = 5$

Synergistic use of the mix will deliver an SCA

Development of the right marketing mix will depend upon:

- Number of differing segments targeted
- Stage of the product life cycles reached
- The industry context, i.e. B2C or B2B
- Need to be consistent
- Resources of the organization
- Corporate and marketing objectives

Marketing Budgets

- *Bottom-up budgeting* – is where the budgeting process is developed within the organization and where the activities happen

- *Negotiated budgeting* – is where the process of budget allocation is by negotiation

- *Objectives and task approach* – is where the budget is allocated specifically on the necessity to achieve output, i.e. achievable objectives

- *Incremental budgeting* – is where the budget is based upon an incremental rise on budgetary expenditure per year, in line with predicted growth in the forthcoming year

- *Percentage of sales method* – is where the budget is allocated, based on a percentage of sales from the previous year

- *Competitive parity* – is where the budget is set, based on spending the same percentage as competitors within the same industry

- *Judgemental methods* – this is where budgets are developed, based upon the judgement of managers most directly involved in the future of the business

REMEMBER!

You must be able to describe a budgetary process and evaluate it in context of a given scenario!

The Control Process

Monitoring and control contains four key activities:

1. Development or adjustment of marketing objectives in line with internal and external drivers affecting performance

2. Setting of performance standards, i.e. key measures such as quality, production, sales

3. Evaluating performance, i.e. identifying performance indicators and measures and analysing findings

4. Corrective action, i.e. revised forecasts or sales targets, increasing advertising, etc.

Methods for controlling the marketing plan:

1. Measuring income/expenditure budgets – performance

2. Performance appraisal evaluation, i.e. staff

3. Variance analysis

4. Budgetary control

5. Benchmarking

6. Marketing mix effectiveness

7. Competitor performance

Hints and Tips

■ Ensure you are clear on the differences between corporate, business and marketing objectives and strategies

■ Remember marketing objectives must be SMART – this is essential

■ You are expected to understand the importance of segmentation and the different segmentation options available to you, including linking them to targeting and positioning

■ Part A of the exam paper, which is the mini-case study, often tests different aspects of the marketing planning process

■ Ensure you consider the 7Ps of the marketing mix, not just the 4Ps

■ Do not just describe budgeting, but be prepared to select an appropriate budgetary process for a given scenario. Be able to evaluate effectively

■ Go to www.cimvirtualinstitute.com and www.marketingonline.co.uk for additional support and guidance

PRODUCT

LEARNING OUTCOMES

➡ Understand how products deliver customer value and satisfy customer requirements
➡ Understand the notion of different levels of product
➡ Understand the product life cycle and its effects on the marketing mix
➡ Understand the principles of product policy

Syllabus Reference: 3.2, 3.4–3.6

KEY REVISION POINTS

➡ Understanding the different facets of the product and the various product classifications
➡ Creating a product range within a product life cycle
➡ Managing the product life cycle
➡ The product adoption process

The Product Dimensions

Key Definition – A product is anything that can be offered to a market for attention, consumption, acquisition or use

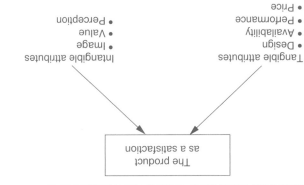

The product as a satisfaction

Tangible attributes
- Design
- Availability
- Performance
- Price

Intangible attributes
- Image
- Value
- Perception

The Five Levels of Product

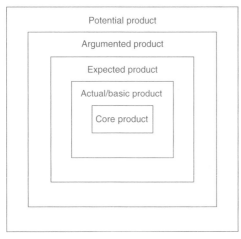

Potential product

Argumented product

Expected product

Actual/basic product

Core product

Core – The basic benefit the product brings, e.g. a car is a form of transport

Actual – Product features such as style and design, e.g. BMW

Expected – The attributes the customer expects the product to deliver, e.g. reliability, status. If these are lacking, the customer will be dissatisfied

Augmented – Additional attributes which support the product and enhance the package, e.g. after sales support, servicing, etc. Often the main area of differentiation

Potential – How the product may evolve, e.g. electric cars

Product classifications

The product has three classifications:

- **Durable** – Products that are durable last for a period of time, e.g. a car's stereo system, a washing machine, etc.
- **Non-durable** – Products that can be consumed or used only once, i.e. food, paper, drinks, etc.
- **Service products** – Services are intangible – there is nothing physical at the end of the service experience, i.e. holidays, hairdressing, personal banking/financial services

Sub-classifications of product classifications

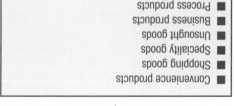

- Convenience products
- Shopping goods
- Specialty goods
- Unsought goods
- Business products
- Process products
- Plant and equipment
- Supplies and services

Creating a Product Range

Components of the product range include the product mix and the product line

- The product mix is the total portfolio of product that a company has to offer

- The product line is a group of closely related products

- Organizations must ensure that they establish the breadth and depth of the product mix

- Organizations should ensure that products are compatible with one another and that they meet the needs of increasingly powerful customers

- The planning process should enable organizations to reflect on their existing product ranges to ensure that the products fit with one another

- The product or service is at the very heart of the organization's existence and a structured and analytical approach must be taken when developing a product range. This must include analysis of market forces, key drivers, factors influencing change and an in-depth understanding of customers

The Product Life Cycle

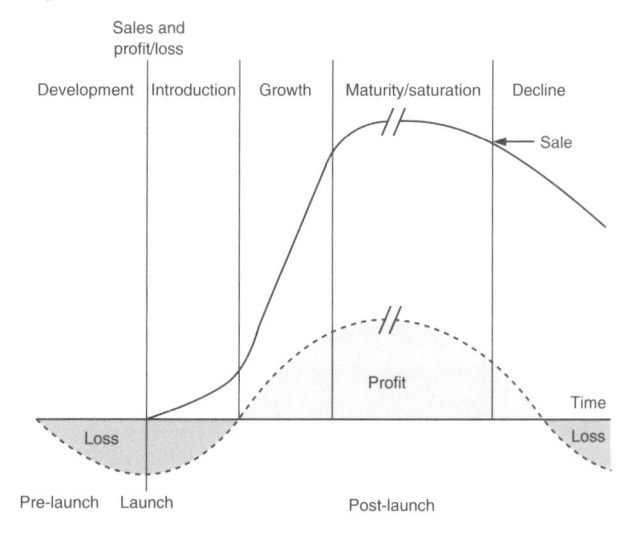

Managing the Product Life Cycle

Marketing strategy for growth

- Introducing new and innovative products
- Undertaking high levels of advertising and sales promotions activity – offering incentives to switch brands
- Targeting customers should be tightly defined
- Marketing mix should be well coordinated and effective

Marketing strategy for maturity

- Modification of the product/services – quality, function and style modifications
- Strategies for differentiation
- Aim for market development and market penetration to maximize profit potential

Marketing strategy for decline

- Consider the introduction of more innovative and up-to-date versions for the same product
- Replacement strategies should be defined
- Carefully manage the decline of the product
- Consider which approach is more appropriate – repositioning or obsolescence
- Consider the three approaches to obsolescence – phase it out, run it out, drop it

Criticisms of the Product Life Cycle

■ Stages not always clearly defined in terms of where one ends and another begins

■ Not all products go through all stages

■ The progression can be changed by strategic decisions such as repositioning

■ Length will vary according to industry sector, e.g. aviation vs. electronic toys

International Product Life Cycle

■ Identified by Lancaster, it is often the case that as a market enters maturity in one country, the organization will decide to export that product to other markets to grow the brand

■ The product then enters the growth stage in that new market

■ However, with the pace of change increasing and global brands becoming more prevalent, many countries may miss out on several stages of a product's evolution

The Product Adoption Process

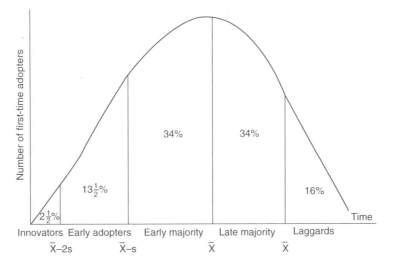

Categories of Adoption

Innovators – Early Adopters

Younger, well educated and high disposable incomes. Like to be the first to have something new. Price is not an issue. Early adopters enter at the growth stage

Early Majority

Slightly above average in terms of education and disposable income. Influenced by the opinion leaders in the Innovator/Early Adopter categories

Late Majority

Adopt innovations after acceptance by the previous groups and usually because of social pressure or because the price has fallen

Laggards

Cautious, older with low disposable income. Last into the market. Often buy when Innovators have moved on to new innovations

The Adoption Process

Awareness

↓

Interest

↓

Evaluation

↓

Trial

↓

Adoption

↓

Post-adoption confirmation

Rate of Diffusion (Degree of Adoption) Dependent Upon:

Communicability – The easier the product benefits can be communicated, the faster the diffusion occurs

Trialability – If it is possible to have a trial before purchase then the faster the diffusion will occur

Relative Advantage – Advantages over and above the products previously marketed. The greater the additional advantages, the faster the diffusion

Branding

> The means of distinguishing one supplier's product from another, by conferring a set of values upon that brand. Often referred to as a bundle of attributes. This can be achieved by:
>
> Name
>
> Packaging
>
> Image
>
> Positioning

Benefits

- Creating a brand creates a vehicle for communication
- Powerful at creating an SCA
- Consumers relate to brands and feel an affinity towards them
- Consumers gain status from buying branded products
- Brands hold power within the distribution process
- Brands are highly valued company assets

Consumers relate to brands due to:

- Emotional connections
- Status benefits
- The ability to lessen the risk of purchasing

Establishing and Supporting Successful Brands

Requires:

> Linking brand values with target customer needs
>
> Determining brand values in relation to those held for competitive brands
>
> Perceptual positioning to be established in line with brand values
>
> Continuous communication of brand values to the target market
>
> Monitor customer perceptions and react to change

Service industry brands are often differentiated on the basis of:

Technical support

Marketing support

Financial support

After-sales support

Often referred to as 'Added value'

Packaging

An effective part of the mix, either as part of the product or as a vehicle for promotion

Packaging design can protect, aid use, communicate and provide convenience to the consumer

Hints and Tips

■ Product operations is an area that is subject to continual questioning in the examinations and it is important to be familiar with it and to be able to apply it

■ Ensure that you can talk competently about the importance of product models when assessing the current status of products within the marketing mix

■ It is important to show that you understand the importance of managing growth at each stage of the product life cycle and the methods and options for doing so

■ Always aim to link other aspects of the marketing mix to the product life cycle and show how each element of the marketing mix applies and contributes to the successful implementation of product/service operations

■ Go to www.cimvirtualinstitute.com and www.marketingonline.co.uk for additional support and guidance

NEW PRODUCT DEVELOPMENT AND PORTFOLIO MANAGEMENT

Unit 4

Syllabus Reference: 3.6, 3.7

Product Portfolio Planning Tools

Portfolio analysis is a collection of techniques aimed at managing a company's collection or portfolio of products.

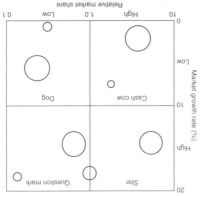

The Boston Consulting Grid (BCG)

The General Electrical Matrix (GE Matrix)

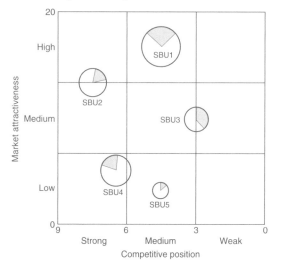

The Shell Directional Policy Matrix

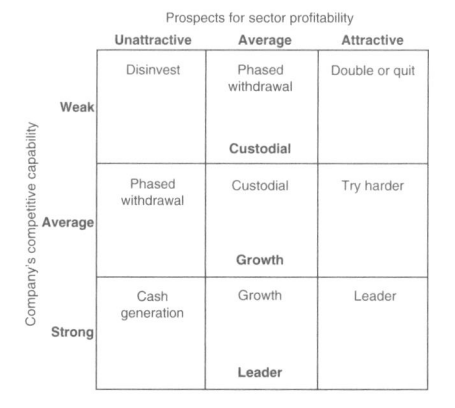

Prospects for sector profitability

	Unattractive	Average	Attractive
Weak	Disinvest	Phased withdrawal **Custodial**	Double or quit
Average	Phased withdrawal	Custodial **Growth**	Try harder
Strong	Cash generation	Growth **Leader**	Leader

Company's competitive capability

These three are commonly used and all look at the attractiveness or growth potential in the market and the ability of the organization's brands to compete in the market

All of these models are concerned with the stage of life that the product is in and the strategies available. These can be summarized by using the model to the right

Product Life Cycle Portfolio Matrix

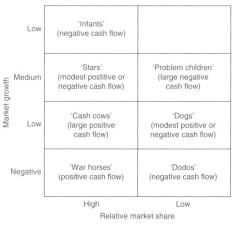

Low	'Infants' (negative cash flow)	
Medium	'Stars' (modest postitive or negative cash flow)	'Problem children' (large negative cash flow)
Low	'Cash cows' (large positive cash flow)	'Dogs' (modest positive or negative cash flow)
Negative	'War horses' (positive cash flow)	'Dodos' (negative cash flow)
	High	Low

Market growth

Relative market share

New Product Development

Different types of new product development

New World/Innovation

The focus of this model is upon technical development, incurring high/risk return. Can revolutionize or create markets

New product lines or additions

Such products can be (i) new to the provider or (ii) be additions to the product range

Product revisions/replacements

Replacements and upgrades of existing products. Changes can be aimed at cost reductions

Reposition

Aim to diversify away from existing markets by uncovering new applications, uses or markets for current products

Imitative products

Copycat products produced by others, but where there is a market for many alternative and competing versions

The New Product Development Process

Idea generation – From market research or gleaned from the market via sales people. Ideas generated should be collected via a management function

Screening – Size of potential market, real consumer need, company's competence and resources

Testing – Various concepts via market research with potential customers

Business analysis – Will it pay? Does it add value to the portfolio?

Product development – Prototype developed, researched and fine-tuned

Test marketing – Launching the product in a smaller area, representative of the total population, irons out final problems before wide-scale investment

Launch – All criteria examined and full launch planned

Highest chance of success is 50%

Costs of New Product Development

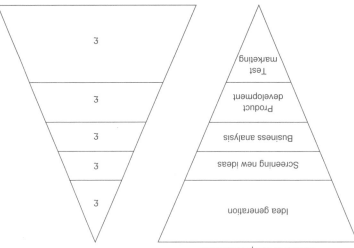

Number of new product ideas

Idea generation

Screening new ideas

Business analysis

Product development

Test marketing

How ICT can aid NPD

Interactive nature of the Internet can involve the customer at an earlier stage

Databases can be used to identify potential customers and involve them at the early stages

Concepts and ideas can be shown and research obtained on potential customer reaction

Computer-aided design shortens the process to prototype

International NPD

International NPD requires products that meet international legal requirements

Economies of scale are apparent as the potential market size is multiplied

Joint ventures/strategies and alliances often take place, to reduce risk and increase skill base in international markets

Hints and Tips

- Ensure that you can talk competently about the importance of product portfolio models when assessing the current status of products within the marketing mix

- New product development and the process that an organization goes through when considering NPD, is often an exam question in Part B of the Marketing Fundamentals paper

- How ICT underpins and aids marketing processes is also often part of Part B questions

- Go to www.cimvirtualinstitute.com and www.marketingonline.co.uk for additional support and guidance

PRICE OPERATIONS

Unit 5

➡ Understand the role and importance of price in the marketing mix
➡ Appreciate the process of making pricing decisions and the internal and external factors affecting these
➡ Understand the different pricing policies

Syllabus Reference: 3.8, 3.9

➡ Price perception of the customer and the organization
➡ Influences on price
➡ Correlating price with value
➡ Determining price
➡ Pricing objectives and strategies

Price – The monetary value placed upon a product/service by the marketer

Cost is only one element, can also be:

Fee   Commission

Interest charged   Time given

Rent

Price is the element of the marketing mix that generates revenue

Revenue = Price $\times$ Quantity

Profit = Revenue – Cost of production

Price can communicate quality

Price can deliver a competitive advantage

Price can build barriers to other market entrants

Price perceptions – the customer and the organization

Customer Perspective

- Price is the value placed upon either a product or a service

- Price is often perceived as being constant, but the reality is that it changes in the mind of the customers as and when their circumstances change

- Supply and demand of products can affect perception, as competitive rivalry and product rarity influence their perception

Organization Perspective

- Price is the only element of the marketing mix that generates revenue for the organization

- Pricing is an opportunity to gain 'ROI' (Return on Investment) or 'ROCE' (Return on Capital Employed)

- Price is used as a means to an end in meeting profit objectives and funding growth opportunities in future years

Key Definitions

Total Cost = The sum of all fixed costs and variable costs times the quantity produced

Average Cost = Total cost divided by the number of units produced

Fixed Costs = Costs that do not vary with the number of units produced or sold

Variable Costs = Costs that vary directly according to the number of units produced or sold

Marginal Cost = The addition to cost of producing one extra unit of output

Economies of Scale = The potential reduction in average costs as a result of increasing output/sales

Contribution = Selling price − Variable cost. This is then a contribution to covering fixed costs

Break-even Point = Fixed costs divided by the level of contribution per unit = number of units that need to be sold before becoming profitable

Customer Demand

The marketer needs to know the amount that will be demanded for differing price levels

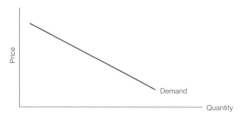

Goods are said to be price inelastic when, regardless of price increase, the customer still purchases the same amount. This often happens in categories where they have no choice, e.g. electricity, car insurance

Goods are price elastic when an increase in price leads to a decrease in demand and vice versa. Most FMCG goods fall into this category

Correlating Price with Value

Typical factors that affect perceived value include:

Life cycle of the product
Product benefits
Product functionality
Quality of the product
Ease of use
Ease of access of the product/service

Value-added measures
Differentiation
Packaging
Positioning
Service and technical support
Competitive alternative

Four Cs that determine price = Customers, Competitors, Company considerations and price as a Communicator

Strategic Pricing Determinants

Demand
This relates to being able to meet customer demand in a cost-effective way

Price senstitivity
Frequency of purchase
Necessity of purchase
Cost of purchase
Competitor alternatives
Stock availability

Debtors and creditors
Liquidity
Credibility
Payment/terms and cashflow
Financial management linked to Key Performance
Indicators (KPIs)

Product positioning
Product perception vs. price
Product value
Price, profitability and product life cycle

Competitors
Match the price of competitors
Reduce price below competitors
Introduce promotional incentives to affect competitors

Other factors
Saturation of markets
Price as a tool for competitive attack
Price vs. value

Pricing Objectives

Pricing objectives include:

- **To achieve return on investment** – ensuring sufficient sales revenue to cover all associated cost bases and pay back initial investment

- **To maximize profits** – setting prices for profitability, i.e. low market share may mean high price to maximize profit potential

- **To maximize sales revenue** – increase sales turnover – selling volume leading to increased profitability

- **To achieve product quality leadership** – providing the best quality product in the market in order to create differentiation against competitors

- **To survive in the market place** – setting objectives that ensure survival in a highly competitive market is central to organizational success. However, organizations tend to aim higher than survival. The aim is to work on a break-even basis in order to stay in business

Strategic Pricing

Price Skimming

Charging high prices to gain early return on investment

Price skimming features include:

- Relatively high price per unit
- Good strategy to apply to new products to recoup costs
- Easy to segment the market
- Profits can be made on a per unit basis

Price Penetration

Charging a low price to ensure market penetration

Price penetration features include:

- Offers a low price per unit
- Is used when a large volume of market share is involved
- Profit is made through volume of sales
- Low price is aided by high promotions

Tactical Pricing

Characteristics of tactical pricing strategies include:

1. *Marginal pricing*

Offering a special price
Ensuring profit is still made

2. *Quantity discounting*

Economies of scale
Money is received quickly
Removing chances for the competition to penetrate the market, by offering bulk buys

3. *Differential pricing*

High fixed costs
The relevant application of seasonal timings
Benefits both the producer and the consumer

4. *Cost-plus pricing*

Covering the cost of overheads, plus percentage on top, to meet marketing/profit objectives
Often used for projects that are difficult to cost out or take a long time for completion

Other Pricing Strategies

Perceived value price

Most are marketing orientated, in that price is related to the perceived value and set at what the markets will bear. Other elements of the mix are used to build high quality perception

Psychological pricing

Perceptual tactics £10 or £9.99 – one says a bargain, the other quality

Segmented/differential pricing

Allows pricing to flex dependent upon demand over time, e.g. off-peak travel

Promotional pricing

Variety of tactics including

Cash rebates or sales promotions

Special event pricing

Lost leader pricing

Low interest deals

Product mix pricing

Where the pricing for related items is also important, i.e. razors and razor blades, where one is sold at a loss to generate profitable sales for the other

Establishing a Price – A Structured Approach

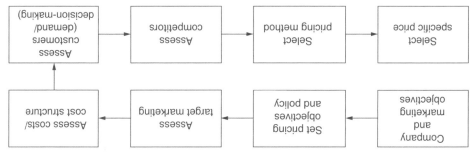

Hints and Tips

■ The price element of the marketing mix should aim to blend price, quality and perceived value

■ Price is the only element of the mix that creates income for the organization

■ Demonstrate your understanding and show that customers are fickle; they have considerable choice and therefore have a significant influence on supply and demand

■ Prices will vary according to what people will pay and also what they are prepared to pay. Therefore, pricing needs to be used with some flexibility to meet those requirements. You should be able to show how you might achieve this level of flexibility

■ The critical success factors in relation to price are to maintain the organization objectives, whilst at the same time remaining sensitive to customer needs

■ The key to price is to link the product quality with a clear indication of value for money. Pitch the price at the right level – it may be the difference between success and failure

■ Go to www.cimvirtualinstitute.com and www.marketingonline.co.uk for additional support and guidance

PLACE OPERATIONS

Unit 6

LEARNING OUTCOMES

➡ Appreciate the process of designing channels of distribution, including the factors that affect decisions in this area

➡ Be aware of the key trends and developments in distribution, including those from use of ICT

Syllabus Reference: 3.10, 3.11

KEY REVISION POINTS

➡ Influences on distribution

➡ The role and benefits of intermediaries

➡ The distribution channel and the customer

➡ Selecting channels of distribution and intermediaries

➡ Vertical and horizontal channel integration, and PDM

➡ Evaluating channel effectiveness

Key Influences on Distribution

There is a wealth of influences, both internal and external, in relation to distribution or 'place' as a tool of the marketing mix. The list is extensive. Try to select a number of influences that you may be confident and comfortable in discussing

- Fuel prices
- Environmental legislation
- Taxation
- Transportation
- National/global transportation infrastructure
- Packaging
- Product life cycle
- Nature and characteristics of the product
- Changing lifestyles
- The emergence of ICT
- Customer wants and expectations
- Level of complexity in buying behaviour
- Competitive strategies
- Production targets
- Marketing mix components
- Customer services
- Technical support

> **Place is about getting the goods to the customer**
>
> **Right Place**
>
> **Right Time**
>
> **Right Quantity**
>
> **Right Condition**
>
> **Right Level of Support**

Marketing Channels

Marketing Channels need to be evaluated in relation to the cost of use and the competitive advantage they can
deliver

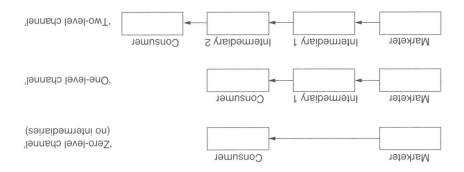

Marketer		Consumer	'Zero-level channel' (no intermediaries)
Marketer	Intermediary 1	Consumer	'One-level channel'
Marketer	Intermediary 1	Intermediary 2	Consumer	'Two-level channel'

Key Factors

Channel length

See the diagram on page 72. The longer the channel length, the greater the loss of control the marketer has

Types of Intermediaries

Agents and brokers – often used internationally

Distributor and dealers – independents who form alliances with manufacturers and add value, e.g. cars

Wholesalers – buy in bulk and sell on in smaller chunks

Retailers – closest to point of purchase – buy from wholesalers or direct

Market Coverage

Intensive – Maximum cover, all outlet types

Selective – More specialist retailers required, e.g. cars

Exclusive – Expensive items convey quality, e.g. Rolex

Channel Management/Responsibility

Who has the ultimate control?

Who sets price?

Who holds title to the goods?

Who is responsible for quality?

Who provides after-sales support and warranty?

The Distribution Channel and the Customer

Passing of goods and services directly from the manufacturer to the consumer

Passing of goods and services via a retailer and then on to a consumer

From the manufacturer via a wholesaler and then directly on to the consumer

The passing of goods and services from the manufacturer via a wholesaler, then on to the retailer and subsequently the consumer

The manufacturer can distribute the products and services via an agent to a wholesaler

Selecting the Channels of Distribution

Below is a list of key questions that marketers should ask when aiming to select the most appropriate distribution channels:

- What are the product characteristics and how do they affect methods of distribution?
- Who are the customers and where are they?
- What are the customer requirements in relation to access and delivery of their products and services?
- How, where and when do they want to buy their products?
- What are their competitors doing by way of distribution?
- What is the cost of distribution?
- What are the legal and regulatory constraints on distribution?

Intermediary Selection Criteria

Operational Criteria

Knowledge of local markets

Appropriate premises and equipment

Technological systems and processes

Customer convenience

Product knowledge and expertise

Payment facilities

Sales force structure, size and effectiveness

Efficient customer service infrastructure

Strategic Criteria

Plans for growth and expansion

Resource capacity and future development

Quality assurance processes

Management ability

Innovative

Willing partnership

Levels of loyalty and cooperation

Channel Strategies

Intensive Distribution

Maximum number of outlets
Target outlets in as many geographical regions
as possible
Consumer convenience products
High purchase frequency
Impulsive purchase
Low price

Selective Distribution

Medium level of customers
Less intensive distribution outlet
Shopping-based products
Medium number of shoppers
Purchase is occasional
Purchase is more likely to be planned
Medium price

Exclusive Distribution

Relatively few customers
Limited retail outlets
Closer retailer/customer relationships
Speciality products
Infrequent purchase
High involvement and planned purchase
High price

Vertical, Horizontal and Physical Distribution Management (PDM)

Vertical Distribution

A distribution system where two or more channel members are connected by ownership or legal obligation

or

A marketing channel in which a single channel member will coordinate or manage channel activities to achieve efficient, low-cost distribution, aimed at satisfying target market customers

Horizontal Distribution

The combination of institutions at the same level of channel operation under one management

Physical Distribution Management (PDM)

This is the term used to describe the management of every part of the distribution process. This can be contracted out to a specialist, or can be developed as a specialist function within the organization

Things to consider:

■ Costs involved
■ Methods of transport
■ Routes used
■ Stock and storage
■ Protection and delivery of stock
■ Timing – a key element

The Internet and Distribution

The benefits of the Internet at a strategic level

Improves corporate image

Improves customer service

Increases visibility

Creates market growth opportunities

Lowers overall business costs

Moves towards online transactions

The benefits of the Internet at an operational level

Improves speed of transaction

Improves management information

Increased service levels

Removal of time constraints

Removal of distance

Ability to complete transactions electronically

Access to full competitive arena

New revenue opportunities

Cost-effectiveness

Evaluating Channel Effectiveness

Key performance and evaluation measures include:

- Regular reviews
- A forum for problem review and solution
- Monthly, quarterly and yearly sales data analysis
- Average stock levels
- Lead and delivery times
- Zero defects
- Customer service complaints
- Marketing support
- Annual performance audits

From an Internet perspective, typical evaluation methods include:

- Number of leads
- Increased sales
- Customer retention
- Increased market share
- Brand enhancement and loyalty
- Customer service

Hints and Tips

- There is an increasing emphasis on distribution. Ensure that the key concepts of intermediaries, channels and channel selection criteria are clear in your mind

- Be prepared to make a decision on channel options, based upon clear justifications of choice

- Ensure that you are confident with the broader complexities of distribution, the challenges, costs, logistical arrangements and how they must be managed to meet different channel stakeholders

- There is increasing evidence of mergers and acquisitions closely related to distribution economies

- Be confident in your ability to discuss new emerging alternatives to distribution, in particular various e-technologies that support and underpin the distribution process

- Channel management and channel selection is a key marketing activity and it is important to ensure that you can find new and innovative ways of meeting customer needs and wants

- Go to www.cimvirtualinstitute.com and www.marketingonline.co.uk for additional support and guidance

PROMOTIONAL OPERATIONS

Unit 7

LEARNING OUTCOMES

➡ Understand the role and importance of communication and promotion in marketing
➡ Understand the process of communication
➡ Understand the range of tools that comprise the marketing communications mix
➡ Understand the factors that contribute to the development and implementation of the marketing communications mix
➡ Be aware of key trends and developments in promotion

Syllabus Reference: 3.12

KEY REVISION POINTS

➡ The marketing communications mix in the context of marketing planning
➡ Push and pull strategies
➡ Aims and objectives of the promotional communications process
➡ The promotional mix

Promotional Operations

It is essential that customers are aware of the products/services that are provided and the way in which they differ from those of competitors

The customers are informed via the use of promotion or marketing communications

The promotional element of the marketing mix is very costly and it is therefore essential that the company:

Sends the correct message

To the correct audience

Using the most appropriate media

The communication process

Individuals are bombarded by thousands of messages every day. A look at the process of communication demonstrates why all are not remembered. Communication involves:

Sender – the person or company wishing to communicate a message

Encoding – translating the message into signs and symbols that the receiver will understand and react positively to

Channel – chosen media to transmit the message, e.g. television or a direct mail letter

Receiver – the person to whom the message was intended, usually the customer

Decoding – the content of the message received by the receiver can differ from the one sent

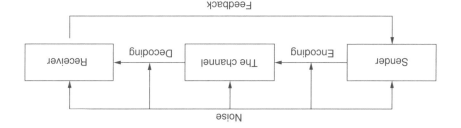

Noise goes on around us all the time in daily life. Promotional messages have to cut through that noise to be heard

Feedback from the receiver can be in many forms – additional sales, complaints or general reaction to the campaign

Customer Behaviour Models

In order to communicate well, we need to understand how people behave when they are purchasing

Response Hierarchy Models

Attention ⟶ Interest ⟶ Desire ⟶ Action

Attention ⟶ Interest ⟶ Evaluation ⟶ Trial ⟶ Adoption ⟶ Post-adoption confirmation

Unawareness ⟶ Awareness ⟶ Comprehension ⟶ Conviction ⟶ Action

Push and Pull Strategies

Push Strategy – This is where the manufacturer takes the decision to concentrate their communication efforts on members of the distribution channel. The basis of this strategy is to promote directly to the suppliers, therefore pushing the products down the line to reach the customers throughout various channel members

Pull Strategy – This strategy operates in contrast to the push strategy and requires the manufacturer to create demand for the product through direct communication with the customers. The aim is to create demand at the direct supply end and pull the product upwards through the channels, through customer demand

Five key communication effects of promotional activities

- *Category needs* – the perception of the actual customer needs

- *Brand awareness* – the ability of the consumer to identify and associate with a particular brand

- *Brand attitude* – this relates to the consumer's particular observations, view and perceptions of the brand, cognitive beliefs

- *Brand purchase* – once the category needs have been identified, the brand purchase intention follows

- *Purchase facilitation* – the organization needs to ensure the product is in the right place, at the right price, at the right time

Possible communication objectives

- Clarification of customer needs
- Increasing brand awareness
- Increasing product knowledge
- Improving brand image
- Increasing brand preference
- Stimulating search behaviour
- Increasing trial purchase
- Increasing financial position
- Increasing flexibility of the corporate image
- Increasing cooperation from trade
- Enhancing the reputation of the organization

Based on Delozier – 1976

The Promotional Mix

Advertising – A paid form of non-formal communication that is transmitted through mass media, such as television, radio, newspapers, magazines, direct mail, public transport vehicles, outdoor displays and the Internet

Advertising objectives

- Promoting products, organizations and services
- Stimulating demand for products
- Increasing sales growth
- Educating the market
- Increasing product/service usage
- Reminding/reinforcing
- Reducing demand fluctuations

Advertising and the marketing mix

As a marketing communications planner, you will be involved in the following:

- Liaising with channel members
- Have an awareness of channel needs and the associated communications support
- Provide consistency for all communications and ensure that all members are empowered by the message

Sales Promotions

Sales Promotions – A range of tactical marketing techniques designed within a strategic marketing framework to add value to a product or service in order to achieve specific sales and marketing objectives

Aims and objectives of sales promotions

- To increase brand and product awareness
- To increase trial and adoption of products
- To attract customers to brands
- To level fluctuations in supply and demand
- To disseminate information
- To encourage trading up to next size

Sales promotions and the marketing mix

Responsibility for sales promotions will include:

- Selecting appropriate promotional techniques
- Trade promotions, retailer to consumer promotions, manufacturer to consumer promotions
- Development of consumer loyalty schemes

Public Relations

> **Public Relations** – Is a planned and sustained effort to establish and maintain goodwill and mutual understanding between an organization and its target publics

Aims and objectives of public relations

- To create and maintain the corporate and brand image and enhance the position and standing of the organization in the eyes of the public
- To communicate the organization's ethos and philosophy, and corporate values
- To undertake damage limitation to overcome poor Public Relations (PR)
- To raise the company profile and forge stronger relationships

Responsibility for public relations includes

- Changing negative into positive, hostility into sympathy, prejudice into acceptance, apathy into interest, ignorance into knowledge
- Define techniques such as press releases, press conferences, publications, media relations, etc.
- Undertake internal PR activities
- Select appropriate PR techniques based upon suitability, feasibility and acceptability

Direct and Interactive Marketing

> **Direct and Interactive Marketing** – An interactive system of marketing which uses one or more advertising media to effect a measurable response at any location

Aims and objectives of direct marketing

- Increasing direct mail order levels from new and existing customers
- To increase provision of information to aid information and adoption
- Increase the number of sales leads generated
- Increase the number of trial leads

Responsibilities of direct marketing

- Ensuring an appropriate database that is effective in reaching targets
- Defining the appropriate techniques, e.g. direct mail, Internet, e-mail marketing, tele-marketing, direct response advertising
- To be aware of data protection legislation and how it affects the activities of direct marketing

Sponsorship

Sponsorship – Is the provision of financial or material support by a company for some independent activity … not usually directly linked to the company's normal business, but support from which the sponsoring company would hope to benefit

Sponsorship Objectives

■ Increasing brand awareness

■ Building and enhancing corporate image

■ Raising awareness of brands related to products restricted in advertising through various legislation, such as alcohol and cigarettes

Responsibilities of Sponsorship

■ Selecting appropriate form of sponsorship, i.e. programme sponsorship, arts/sports sponsorship, event sponsorship, individual or team sponsorship

■ To ensure appropriate sponsorship arrangements are in place and the match between the organization and the potential sponsoring organization is right

■ Develop the right mix, i.e. ensuring high-level of spin-offs in promotions, optimizing cost effectiveness, advertising, merchandising and promotional incentives

Personal Selling

Personal Selling – An interpersonal communication tool which involves face-to-face activities undertaken by individuals, often representing an organization, in order to inform, persuade or remind an individual or group to take appropriate action, as required by the sponsor's representative

Objectives of personal selling

- To increase sales turnover
- To reduce the number of clients with minimum viable orders
- To reduce the costs of sales
- To increase the number of distribution outlets

Responsibilities of the marketer in supporting the sales team:

- Provision of market information and competitor intelligence
- Provision of potential leads
- Client history/database information
- Financial reports – Dunn and Bradstreet
- Provision of appropriate promotional materials
- Provision of sales aids, promotional plans and incentives

The promotional planning process

Identify target audience

↓

Set promotional objectives

↓

Determine the message

↓

Set the promotional budget

↓

Determine the promotional mix

↓

Measurement and control of promotional effectiveness

Factors affecting the promotional mix

Target market – lifestyle and media consumption

Characteristics and effectiveness of the tools – in relation to reaching your target audience

Company resources and objectives – launching products requires more resource than maintaining them

Availability of promotional tools

Product life cycle stage

Hints and Tips

■ Ensure that you can link the organization perspective of the marketing mix with the customer perspective

■ Push and pull strategies are commonplace and you should be prepared to include them in potential strategy development areas

■ As for the promotional mix, be familiar with each aspect of the mix, its definition, the objectives the mix can achieve and understand the areas of responsibility that an operational manager should be involved in planning and implementing

■ Be aware of the need to coordinate the promotional mix and ensure that you develop an effective and creative message that will maximize the potential impact of a fully coordinated mix

■ Ensure you are able to apply these areas – it is not knowledge regurgitation

■ Have a go at as many past exam questions as possible

■ Go to www.cimvirtualinstitute.com and www.marketingonline.co.uk for additional support and guidance

SERVICES AND CUSTOMER CARE

Unit 8

LEARNING OUTCOMES

→ Understand the importance of service as an element of the marketing mix

→ Understand the factors that contribute to the delivery of service quality

→ Understand the relationship between service quality and the broader concept of customer care

→ Understand the role and importance of customer care

→ Understand customer care and how to plan and implement a customer care policy

→ Understand the importance of people and a company's staff in contributing to customer care and effective service delivery

KEY REVISION POINTS

→ The management concept of Total Quality Management (TQM)

→ The extended marketing mix

→ Implementing customer care programmes

→ The SERVQUAL model and its application

Services and Customer Care

- The process of adding value to the customer purchase
- Now as applicable to purchasing products as originally a part of service delivery
- Part of the Augmented Product offering
- Enables a sustainable competitive advantage (SCA) to be delivered
- Needs to emanate from a customer-oriented organization

Service is important because of

- Perishability
- Intangibility
- Inseparability

Leads to the application of the extended mix

- **Process** – How the customer actually receives or purchases the goods/services and how effective that transaction is
- **Physical evidence** – The organizational mission and the way it is communicated and manifests itself in the customer transaction
- **People** – The staff the customers encounter, either at the point of purchase or as an after-sales experience

Total Quality Management (TQM)

A management culture that puts quality and customer care at the heart of the organization

TQM approach is to meet customer requirements first time, every time

TQM delivers the quality aspect, whereas customer care delivers the service aspect of the customer experience

TQM – The guiding principles

- Recognition of the strategic importance of customers and suppliers
- Development of win – win relations between customer and suppliers
- Establishing relationships based on trust

These are put into practice by

- Constantly collecting information on customer expectations
- Disseminating the information widely within the organization
- Using the information to design and deliver the product/service offering

TQM needs

- Total commitment from staff
- A customer-orientated culture
- An understanding of customer requirements and the organization's obligations
- Commitment from top management
- Adherence to process and procedures designed to deliver the obligations
- Monitoring of customer needs and how they may change

Information must be

- Up-to-date
- Reliable
- Used to inform decision-making and planning
- Produced to inform and motivate staff
- Produced at regular stages to monitor improvement
- Able to make measurement part of the implementation process

Building a customer care programme

Key questions

What policy of customer care is most appropriate for the company?

How far should this policy affect the operations?

All customers have the right to

- A basic minimum level of customer care
- Common courtesy from staff
- Effective response to complaints

The Customer Care Process

Identify customer needs and perceptions

↑

Establish mission statements service levels and specifications

↑

Establish and communicate management processes and define tasks according to time scales

↑

Establish a basic minimum level of care

↑

Ensure systems for effective response to complaints

↑

Secure management commitment

Successful customer care programmes

Staff must be

- Clear about the programme and their role in it
- Committed to the programme
- Well trained to carry out the programme
- Sufficiently resourced
- Sufficiently skilled

The programme must

- Provide clear benefits for the staff
- Be reinforced with top management commitment and rewards

Management must be

- Informed about the progress and the effectiveness of staff performance
- Provided with regular and appropriate information
- Supportive of marketing objectives and facilitate the work of staff towards meeting those objectives

Benefits

- Minimizes organizational confusion
- Potentially delivers an SCA
- Offers value addition to customers
- Promotes better customer understanding
- Motivates staff
- Aids customer retention

The SERVQUAL Model

As developed by Parasuraman, Zeithaml and Barry

Provides a comprehensive framework for identifying key criteria for the customer

Guides the implementation of quality programmes

Gaps occur because companies

Don't understand what customers want

Are unwilling to provide what they need

Do not have staff trained to meet the needs

May have encouraged unrealistic customer expectations

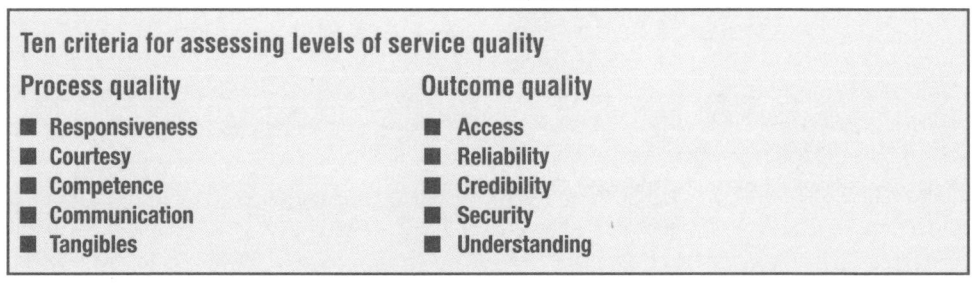

Ten criteria for assessing levels of service quality

Process quality

- Responsiveness
- Courtesy
- Competence
- Communication
- Tangibles

Outcome quality

- Access
- Reliability
- Credibility
- Security
- Understanding

Hints and Tips

■ Ensure that you fully understand the benefits that customer care can deliver

■ Ensure that you are aware of the process of building a customer care system and the commitment required from the organization

■ Ensure that you have an understanding of the SERVQUAL model and are able to apply it to a range of organizations

■ Build up a set of examples from your own experience of good and bad customer service to use as examples in the exam

■ Go to www.cimvirtualinstitute.com and www.marketingonline.co.uk for additional support and guidance

MARKETING IN CONTEXT

LEARNING OUTCOMES

← Understanding the importance of contextual setting in influencing the selection of the marketing mix tools

← Understand the differences in the characteristics of various types of marketing context

← Being able to compare and contrast the marketing activities of organizations that operate and compete within different contextual settings

← Understand some of the key contextual factors affecting the marketing mix, such as ICT, international dimensions

KEY REVISION POINTS

← The importance of the contextual setting on the development of the marketing mix

← Understanding the different contextual settings that exist

← Understanding the role of ICT in further development of marketing orientation

← Understanding the importance of international markets

Syllabus Reference: 3.3, 3.15, 4.1–4.5

Marketing in Differing Contexts

Fast Moving Consumer Goods or B2C – Buyer Decision-making Process (DMP)

Problem recognition

↓

Information search

↓

Evaluation of alternatives

↓

Purchase decision

↓

Post-purchase behaviour

Buyer behaviour (DMP) is dependent upon

Personal factors – Age, sex, economic profile and family life stage. Also level of involvement in purchase category

Psychological factors – Perceptions, motivations, attitudes and personality and how these affect the purchasing

Social and cultural factors – Who are we heavily influenced by? Who are our opinion leaders and reference groups? How do they influence us?

Business-2-Business markets – DMP

Problem recognition

↓

Develop product specification to solve problem

↓

Supplier search

↓

Supplier evaluation relative to specifications

↓

Supplier selection

↓

Product ordering/purchase

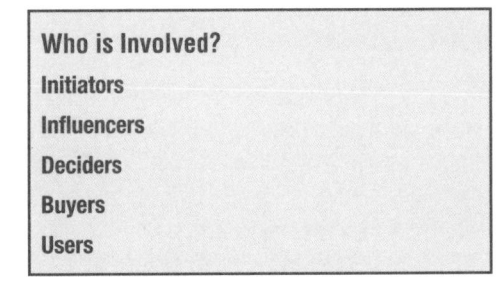

Who is Involved?

Initiators

Influencers

Deciders

Buyers

Users

Factors affecting B2B purchasing

Environmental factors – STEPLE

Interpersonal factors – How the buying unit or DMU relate to each other and work together

Organizational factors – Such as inviting to tender

Individual factors – Personal preferences

FMCG markets	Business-to-business markets
Buyer/buying situations	
Individual/family	Group/organizational
Personal motives	Organizational requirements
Often unplanned/less rational	Planned/rational
Not specialist buyer	Trained/professional
Less informed	Well informed
Little power	Substantial power
Marketing mix product	
Often standardized	Often customized
Less technical	More technical
Less service	More service
Price	
Less important	More important
Rarely negotiated	Frequently negotiated
Few tenders/bids	Often tenders/bids
Promotion	
Emphasis on non-personal	Emphasis on personal
Place	
Less direct	Usually direct
Logistics important	Logistics vital

Small to medium enterprises (SME)

Although small, these organizations will need to be more marketing oriented in order to compete with larger organizations in their sector, they will typically have restrictions on resources affecting:

- Staff numbers and skills
- Financial resources
- Information access
- Systems

Many SMEs form alliances to share resources, such as marketing research information and utilize Government services such as Business Link

Service sector

Service		Physical products
High ◄——— Perishability ———►		Low
High ◄——— Intangibility ———►		Low
High ◄——— Inseparability ———►		Low
High ◄——— Variability ———►		Low
No ◄——— Ownership ———►		Yes

Key Issues:

Perishability

Intangibility

Variability

Inseparability

Non-ownership

E-Commerce or E-Business

> **Key Definition – The use of electronic technologies and systems, so as to facilitate and enhance transactions between different parts of the value chain**

Can deliver

Cost reductions to the marketer

Enhanced service to the customer

Covers the use of

Internet – Internally, i.e. Intranet

　　　　　Externally, i.e. Extranet

World Wide Web – as an information source

Electronic Data Interchange (EDI)

Data base technology – data warehousing

　　　　　　　　　　– data mining

Advantages

- Better communication
- Faster and more flexible transactions
- Removal of geographical boundaries
- Better coordination of value chain
- Improved relationships and retention

E-Commerce markets

Travel	Cars	Grocery
Music	Toys	Insurance
Books	Software	
Wine	Event booking	

Digital Technology Enables

Direct response television

Two-way communication

Interactive television

Multimedia – CD Roms/DVDs

Mobile technology

Wireless technology

SMS messaging

E-mails/video clips

All of these developments are able to improve

Quality and quantity of marketing research information for decision-making

Communication between the value chain and the end user, resulting in improved service to the customer

Improvements to the promotional mix, enabling greater measurement and degree of two-way communications

Improved customer management – electronic CRM and customer care, providing quicker, more targeted responses at a cheaper price

The International Marketing Mix

Product

Manufacturing requirements
Market research
Ability to produce the product
Customer needs and fit with the product portfolio
Technical/after-sales support
Technology
Standardization vs. adaptation

Price

Economic variables, currency exchange rates, international and local legislation

Varying taxes, tariffs

Price sensitivity and cultural diversity

Place

Set-up costs of channel members
Level of investment required
Level of incentive required
Synergy with local/domestic channels
Management and control of the overall process

Promotional mix

Language, image, relationships
Corporate identity, company image
Methods of advertising/tolerance of advertising
Media, ethics, literacy, accessibility
Agencies

Standardization

A company wishing to globalize its business needs to consider standardization of the following:

- Market access
- Industry standards
- Technology
- Products/services
- Promotion
- Distribution
- Customer requirements
- Competition
- Communication

Adaptation

A company adapting products/services to market needs will consider the following options:

- Modifying the marketing mix to meet different customer needs
- Adapting products to meet local needs and conditions
- Adapting promotional strategies for each of their strategic business units (SBUs) or products/ strategies
- Avoiding conflict in promotional protocol
- Being aware of price sensitivities, economic instabilities, global pricing

Hints and Tips

■ Whilst international marketing is a subject in its own right, it may not always be separated for the purpose of exam questions. For example, you may be asked to answer a marketing planning question in the context of an international business

■ Be prepared to adapt the marketing mix to any given context – B2C, B2B, SMEs, Not-for-Profit and International

■ Be aware of how technology is improving the marketing process and how this works better in some markets than others. Build a bank of examples from reading the quality press

■ Be prepared to compare and contrast marketing contexts and demonstrate you are aware of how these differences manifest themselves

■ Go to www.cimvirtualinstitute.com and www.marketingonline.co.uk for additional support and guidance